GETTING INTO NATURE™

GETTING INTO NATURE™

Sunflowers

INSIDE AND OUT

Text by Andrew Hipp
Illustrations by Andrea Ricciardi di Gaudesi

The Rosen Publishing Group's
PowerKids Press™
New York

For Paul Berry, who has taught me as much about living as about being a taxonomist.

Published in 2004 in North America
by The Rosen Publishing Group, Inc.
29 East 21st Street, New York, NY 10010

Copyright © 2004
by Andrea Dué s.r.l., Florence, Italy, and
Rosen Book Works, Inc., New York, USA

First Edition

Book Design:
Andrea Dué s.r.l., Florence, Italy

Illustrations:
Andrea Ricciardi di Gaudesi and Alessandro Baldanzi, Studio Stalio
Map by Alessandro Bartolozzi

Scientific advice for botanical illustrations:
Riccardo Maria Baldini

Library of Congress Cataloging-in-Publication Data
Hipp, Andrew.
Sunflowers inside and out / by Andrew Hipp.
    p. cm. — (Getting into nature)
Summary: Examines the stem, root system, leaves, and flowering
heads of a sunflower and describes this unique plant's structure,
growth, flowering, reproduction, and cultivation.
ISBN 0-8239-4210-4 (lib. bdg.)
1. Sunflowers—Juvenile literature. [1. Sunflowers.] I. Title. II. Series.
SB299.S9H56 2004
583'.99—dc22
                                                                    2003015537

Manufactured in Italy by Eurolitho S.p.A., Milan

Contents

The Sunflower Family

Sunflowers can grow to more than 10 feet (3 meters) tall, with leaves as broad as your chest and a head that can be as big around as the face of a bear.

Yet the huge sunflower is in the same family as heath asters, whose heads are smaller than a dime. Sunflowers are also in the same family as blue-flowered chickory, prickly thistles, tiny-flowered goldenrods, dandelions, and daisies.

Sunflowers and 20,000 other plant **species** together form one of the largest plant families in the world, called the **Compositae**, or Asteraceae. Of all the Compositae in the world, none is so widely known as the sunflower.

**Domesticated
sunflower**
(Helianthus annuus)

Sunflower Origins

There are about 50 species of wild sunflower, all of which **evolved** in North America. Some have narrow leaves, and others have broad leaves. Some have hairy stems, while others are smooth. Most sunflower species grow in grasslands or meadows, though some grow in woodlands.

Native Americans first **cultivated** sunflowers thousands of years ago, growing sunflower heads that measured 1 foot (0.3 meters) from edge to edge. European travelers to North America in the 1500s brought sunflowers home with them. In the 1700s, the cultivated sunflower traveled to Russia, where it quickly became important to the making of vegetable oil. Today, about one-quarter of the world's sunflower oil comes from Russia, despite the fact that the sunflower originated in central North America.

N. AMERICA

Sunflowers were first domesticated from their wild ancestor (*Helianthus annuus*) in the Great Plains of the United States. They then spread into Mexico and were taken to Europe.

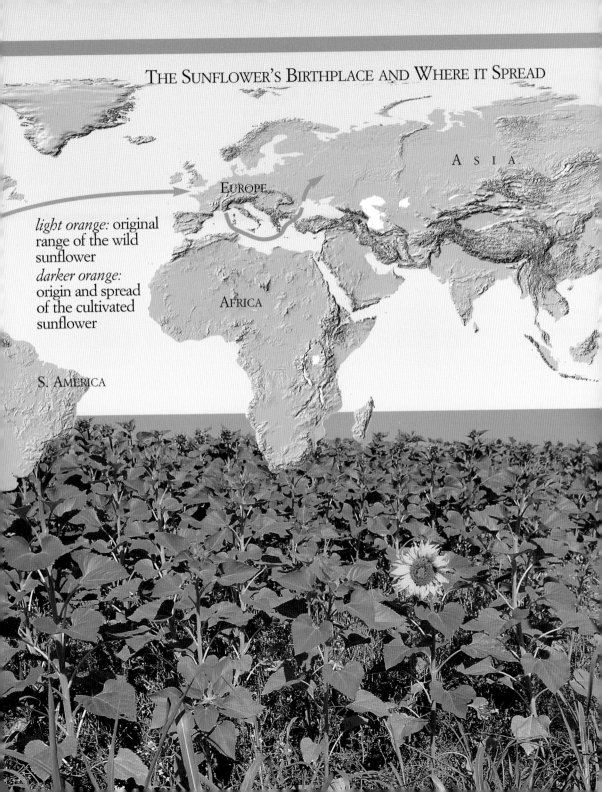

THE SUNFLOWER'S BIRTHPLACE AND WHERE IT SPREAD

ASIA

EUROPE

light orange: original range of the wild sunflower
darker orange: origin and spread of the cultivated sunflower

AFRICA

S. AMERICA

The Body of a Sunflower

Each sunflower begins life as a shoot off of another sunflower or as a seed that is smaller than your fingernail. The sunflower can become twice as tall as a grown person. A sunflower, like most flowering plants, has roots that are covered with root hairs. These hairs absorb, or collect, water and **minerals** from the soil and secure the plant firmly in the ground.

stem

roots

Much of
the food made
by the sunflower's
leaves goes to feed the
growing seeds, filling them
with food to feed the baby
plants. The rest is needed to
produce the roots, leaves, tall
stems, and other parts of
the sunflower body
pictured here.

h e a d

ray flowers

disk

leaves

The stem carries water and minerals
from the roots to all parts of the plant.
It also carries food from the leaves,
which use water, air, and sunlight
to make food through the action
of **photosynthesis**.

9

A Head of Flowers

ray flowers

This is a close-up
of a disk flower.

stigma

phyllaries

anthers

corolla (made up
of five joined petals)

The edge of a sunflower head is ringed
with yellow ray flowers. These ray
flowers on a sunflower head are sterile,
meaning that they do not produce
seeds. All of the other flowers on a
sunflower head are called disk flowers.
The five petals, or leaves, of a disk
flower form a tube called the **corolla**.
The corolla sits on top of an **ovary**, the
part of the flower that produces the seeds.

pappus

ovary

This is a close-up
of a ray flower.

Only disk flowers have ovaries, and only disk flowers can produce sunflower **achenes**. Inside the corolla are **anthers**, which make **pollen**, and a **stigma**, which catches the pollen from other flowers.

disk flowers

When you look at a sunflower or any other member of the Compositae family, the part of the plant that looks like a flower is actually a whole head of flowers. Look closely at the head of a sunflower, dandelion, aster, thistle, or daisy. How many flowers can you count?

Sunflower Pollen

When a disk flower first blooms, or begins to flower, only the anthers can be seen above the rim of the corolla. Anthers are joined along the edges to make a tube, which fills with pollen when the anthers break open. Early on a summer morning, the stigma pushes out through the anther tube, pushing pollen ahead of it. The pollen is collected from the tip of the stigma by bees or other insects and is carried off. The next day, the stigma splits into two curly ends and becomes able to capture pollen from other flowers.

The way that sunflowers have of getting pollen into the world is called pollen presentation. Pollen presentation is a way of making sure that stigmas have a chance to get pollen from other plants. If no pollen is carried to the stigma, the stigma will curl around to touch pollen from its own flower.

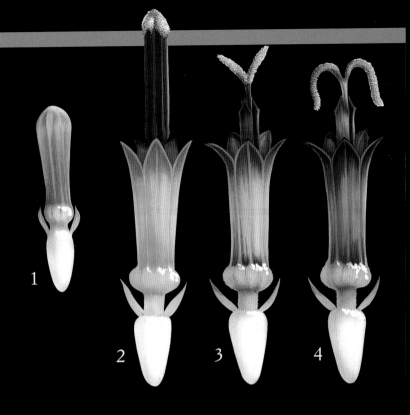

1

2   3   4

Above: The growth stages of a disk flower:

1. A disk flower before blooming.
2. Pollen presentation: the stigma pushes pollen out through the tube of anthers.
3. The stigma opens and can now receive pollen.
4. The stigma opens farther. If it receives no pollen from other sunflowers, it may curl around to touch pollen from the anther tube.

Left: This is a sunflower in full bloom.

13

Making Seeds

Sunflowers get bees to move pollen from one flower to another by making nectar, a sweet liquid that bees use to feed their young and to make honey. As bees collect nectar, they get yellow pollen grains on their bodies. The bees fly from sunflower to sunflower, moving pollen from anthers to open stigmas. This process is called pollination. After a disk flower is pollinated, the pollen produces a long, thin tube that travels down through the stigma into the ovary at the base of the flower. The sunflower pollen and **ovule** each contain half of the instructions needed to make a new sunflower. When the pollen flows through the pollen tube and into the ovule, the two are joined and share their instructions.

This is called fertilization. Once the ovule is fertilized, it grows into a sunflower seed, and the ovary forms the hard outside shell of the sunflower achene.

Most sunflowers depend on pollinators for making seeds. Bees, like the one opposite, are the most important pollinators. When there are not enough bees around, sunflowers produce empty shells that hold no seeds.

14

Sunflower Achenes

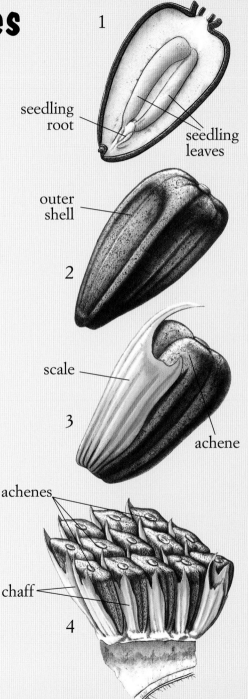

Each fully grown achene has a hard outer shell that surrounds a single seed. Around the seed is a paper-thin wrapping called the seed coat. Each seed has a pointed end and a rounded end. The pointed end is the tip of the seedling root. The rounded end is made up of two seedling leaves, which are packed full of food.

If the seed **germinates**, the young sunflower will live off this food until it is able to make its own food by photosynthesis. Most seeds never germinate, even from wild sunflowers. Birds eat many achenes. Mice collect achenes as well, eating them right away or storing them for later.

1

seedling root

seedling leaves

outer shell

2

scale

3

achene

achenes

chaff

4

Opposite:
1. An inside view
of a sunflower achene.
2. The outer shell of an achene.
3. Each achene is attached to the
sunflower head next to a scale.
4. Together, these scales are called chaff.

Top right: Goldfinches eat thistle,
dandelion, and sunflower
achenes. Mice and some
bird species, such as
chickadees, may either
eat the achenes or store
them for later.

European goldfinch
(Carduelis carduelis)

Bottom right: You can
buy sunflower seeds
and achenes at a store
or market. When
you buy sunflower
"seeds" with the
shells still on, you
are really buying
sunflower achenes.
The seed is hidden
inside the shell.

17

A Sunflower Head from Beginning to End

If you study a sunflower head soon after it opens, you will find disk flowers at the edge that are forming achenes while those in the center have not even opened yet. This is because the disk flowers around the outside edge of a sunflower head grow up first. As the head grows, the petals on its disk flowers begin to fade and dry out. The disk begins to darken, and the head becomes heavy with the growing achenes. At the same time, the back of the head turns from green to yellow as the small leaves that make up the back of the head stop photosynthesizing.

It is often said that sunflower heads turn to face the sun, but this is not entirely true. Growing sunflowers and other green plants often lean toward the sun, whose light they need for photosynthesis.

A growing sunflower head does turn to follow the sun. Once it is in full bloom, however, it slows and stops. It usually ends up facing east. Viewed from left to right, the sunflower on these pages can be seen growing its first achenes, reaching full bloom, and fading at the end of its life.

19

Sunflowers Among Native Americans

Native Americans have long eaten the achenes of wild sunflowers. The wild **ancestor** of the **domesticated** sunflower originated in the Great Plains and followed Indians around North America as a weed for thousands of years. More than 4,000 years ago, Native Americans domesticated the sunflower by planting it in their gardens and singling out plants with large heads and big achenes. The giant sunflower heads were cut from the plants and laid in the sun to dry. The dried heads were then beaten with sticks to free the ripe achenes. The seeds were squashed into paste, beaten, and boiled to release the oil, or cooked over hot coals and ground into flour. Sacks of seeds were often stored for winter food. Some seeds from the largest heads were saved for planting the next year.

Native Americans depended on sunflowers for more than just food. Achenes and yellow ray flowers were used to make dye. Face paint was made from dried petals and pollen. Oil, drawn from ground sunflower seeds by boiling, provided many tribes with cooking oil and hair moisturizer. Sticky sap from the stem was used to treat wounds. Everything from warts to snake bites to sickness due to too much sun could be treated with sunflowers.

Sunflower Weevils

Some insects can harm sunflowers. One example is a kind of beetle called the sunflower seed weevil. In early summer, sunflower seed weevils either poke holes in the shells of growing sunflower achenes and place eggs on the seeds or they place eggs on the disk flowers. The **larvae** that crawl from the eggs feed on oils stored in the seeds. At the end of summer, weevil larvae chew their way through the shell of the achene and drop to the ground. They spend winter in the soil. The next summer, grown weevils crawl out of the soil to lay eggs in a new crop of sunflowers.

A sunflower seed weevil (*left*) will lay eggs in the achenes of sunflowers. The weevil larvae that feed on sunflower seeds can do great harm to entire fields of sunflowers like the one at right.

More than 150 insects feed on North American sunflowers. In central and eastern Europe, there are more than 240 sunflower insect pests.

Sunflowers and Scientists

Sunflowers have taught scientists a great deal about how plants grow and change. Scientists have found, for example, that domesticated sunflowers and their wild relatives often **hybridize**. For example, a domesticated sunflower may provide pollen to a wild sunflower and produce seeds. The seeds produced from hybridization often grow into plants that have features of both the domesticated parent and the wild parent, but sometimes they form plants that are very different from either of the parents. Scientists are also learning more about the lives of sunflower insects. At the same time, they are working on ways to make sunflowers more able to fight insect pests and diseases, or illnesses.

Left: A scientist studies a sunflower in a lab. If you like to be outside and you like sunflowers, you might enjoy being a sunflower scientist yourself. The best way to start is to watch real sunflowers in the field. Learn from a sunflower how it grows. Watch the insects that come to it and what they do when they are on the sunflower. Draw pictures and take notes on what you see.

Opposite, bottom: A grasshopper feeds on a sunflower.

Glossary

achenes (uh-KEENZ) Dry one-seeded fruit.

ancestor (AN-ses-ter) A family member who lived long before those who are alive now.

anthers (AN-thurz) Sacs that hold a plant's pollen. The male, or boy, part of the plant.

Compositae (kum-PAWZ-ih-tee) The plant family that is made of dandelions, sunflowers, daisies, and about 20,000 other species that produce disk flowers and/or ray flowers in heads.

corolla (ko-ROH-luh) A flower's petals, joined along the edges to form a tube.

cultivated (KUHL-tih-vay-ted) Helped to grow, as in a garden.

domesticated (duh-MES-tih-kay-ted) Something that was once wild but has been changed for use by humans.

evolved (ee-VOLVD) Changed or come into existence over the course of many years.

germinates (JER-mi-nates) Begins to grow from a seed.

hybridize (HY-brih-dize) To create seeds in a plant of one species from pollen of a plant of a different species.

larvae (LAHR-vee) Insects in an early stage of life.

minerals (MIH-ner-ulz) Natural substances in the soil, like iron and calcium, many of which are needed by plants.

ovule (OV-yule) The matter inside a plant's ovary that grows up to become a seed following germination.

ovary (OH-vuh-ree) The female, or girl, part of a flower, which grows up to become a fruit.

photosynthesis (foh-toh-SIN-thuh-sis) The process by which green plants use energy from sunlight to turn carbon dioxide (the gas we breathe out) and water into sugar and oxygen.

pollen (PAH-lin) The dustlike material made by seed plants that is carried to other plants to help them flower.

species (SPEE-sheez) A single kind of plant, animal, or other living thing. For example, all people are in the human species.

stigma (STIG-muh) The portion of a flower that catches pollen. Stigmas are connected to ovaries.

Index

Web Sites

Due to the changing nature of Internet links, PowerKids Press has developed an online list of Web sites related to the subject of this book. This site is updated regularly. Please use this link to access the list:

www.powerkidslinks.com/gin/sunf

About the Author

Andrew Hipp has been working as a naturalist in Madison, Wisconsin, since 1993. He is currently finishing his doctoral work in botany at the University of Wisconsin. Andrew and his wife, Rachel Davis, are collaborating on an illustrated field guide to common sedges of Wisconsin as they look forward to the birth of their first child.

Acknowledgments
This book draws on research and ideas of J. M. Burke, L. D. Charlet, J. B. Free, C. B. Heiser, L. H. Rieseberg, A. E. Schwarzbach, and their collaborators. The author gratefully acknowledges Doctors Charlet and Rieseberg for sharing information based on their own research, and Dr. Rieseberg for reviewing a draft of this manuscript.

Photo Credits